I0846107

UNBLOCK YOUR WRITING

33 MOTIVATIONAL MINDSETS TO KICK YOUR CREATIVITY IN THE ASS

UNBLOCK YOUR WRITING
33 motivational mindsets to kick your creativity in the ass

© 2023 by Winther-John Productions. All rights reserved. No part of this book may be used or reproduced in any manner whatsoever without written permission except in the case of brief quotations embodied in critical articles and reviews.

Cover design & layout by Marcus Winther-John

ISBN 9798853465411

Thank you, Henriette Tybjerg, Charlotte Ilsø Andersen, Daniel Winther-John and all my talented students at Danish Songwriting Academy and the Royal Academy of Music.

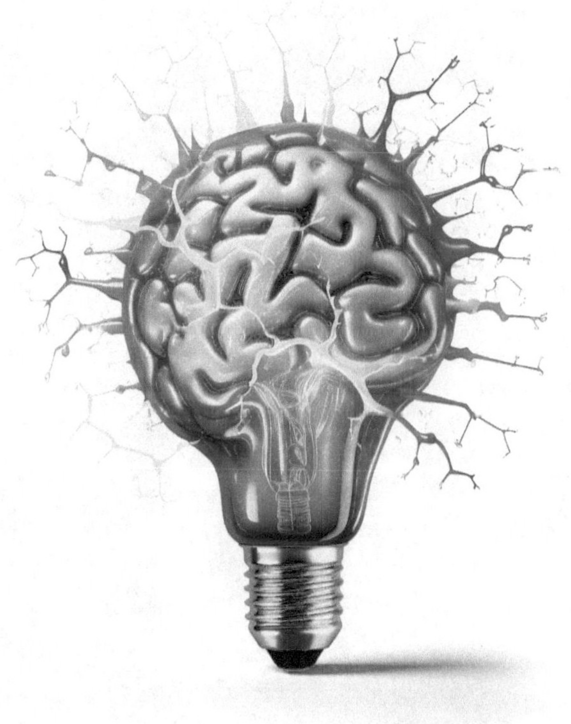

ON THE BLOCK

Introduction
On the block

This book is not only for writers of books or songs. It is for anyone who creates or generates ideas in any form. The more I explore the depths of the creative process and discuss it with colleagues, the clearer it seems that regardless of whether you create with clay, words, melodies, or paint, the characteristics and challenges of the creative process are strikingly similar.

So, just replace the word "write" with whatever you do.

The writer's block most people experience is an accumulated block, built up over time by numerous creative hurdles they could not get past. Writer's block is present in every creative situation as a selection of potential pitfalls and dead ends. A successful creative process is a slalom around these, using a balance of lightness and focus to maintain the momentum.

In that sense, the concept of a whole book drawing attention to and going into detail with these dangers is theoretically counterproductive. But sometimes you need to identify your enemies to defeat them. And the enemies of your productivity, collectively entitled "writer's block", are masters of disguise that sneak in under the pretense of ambition, common sense, logic, high art, originality, etc. These saboteurs are close allies of your ego and are on a mission to stop you from creating.

You are an artist. You should be creating, not reading about creating. Therefore, I have kept the chapters in this book short and to the point. I won't waste your time rephrasing the same thoughts again and again without new points and angles just to fill extra pages. Neither will I go into unnecessary depth, detailing the whys and hows, anecdotes and personal background (but I will definitely be filling other books with all that stuff in the near future).

Some chapters are a kick in the ass, such as "Do your job", "No excuses", and "Don't wait for the perfect time".

Some are intended to help you find a constructive mindset "Be an optimist" and "Don't be the best, do your best", and some are to remind you of the deep satisfaction of serving your art selflessly "Your writing is not you", "Don't be original", and "The whole world doesn't give a shit!".

Some chapters are proactive and practical, "Write something bad!", "Deadlines", and "Take a Walk". And, although I am a great proponent of a hands-on approach to creativity, there are also chapters that zoom out on something more abstract and arty ("Dance with the magic" and "Snapshots from a writer's life").

This is not a step-by-step manual. So, zap around and grab an inspirational snack here and there. Inspiration and creativity come in endless variations, and what gets you going one day may be very different the next.

So, open your mind, jump in …
but for God's sake, do something!

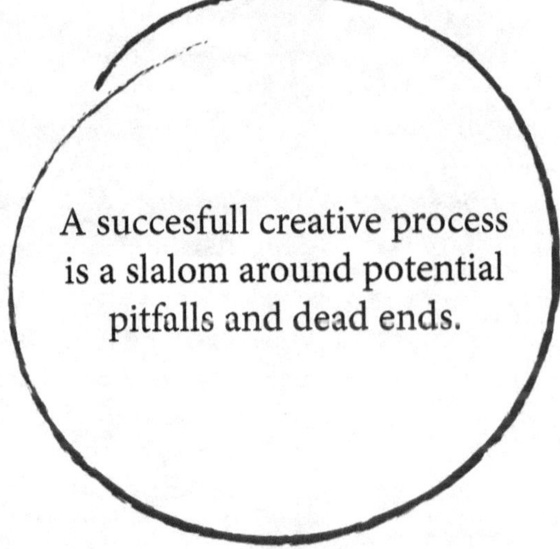

A succesfull creative process
is a slalom around potential
pitfalls and dead ends.

WRITER'S BLOCK DOES NOT EXIST!

No.1
Writer's block does not exist!

… not physically. It is a concept of your own creation, like a song or a story. People who pass you on the street cannot see your writer's block. It cannot block the way of other people. Outside of your mind it does not exist. It is an idea that you made up, and therefore you can also change it and control it.

When you choose to eliminate writer's block, it does not disappear instantly. However, that choice delivers the first blow to the creative monster under the bed. And every proactive creative choice you make from then on will take away more of its power.

IT'S THERE … WHO CARES?

No.2

It's there ...
who cares?

Once you have created writer's block, you have summoned the Candyman. You have opened the bottle and let the genie out. And this is actually okay.

Ideas and creative options are constantly swirling around us, waiting to be picked out of thin air by an artist, writer, musician, or anyone else who is open to them.

Some ideas seem great, some fun, and some bad. Floating around all these ideas are doubts, expectations, insecurities, and excuses—all potential parts of a writer's block.

Acknowledge that these negative thoughts are there and then do not give them any more attention. The more you move your focus to the work in the creative process and deprive writer's block of attention, the more it shrinks and weakens.

DO SOMETHING…
NOW!

No.3
Do something …
now!

Do you want to create or not? If not, then stop wasting time torturing yourself by pretending that you are going to. Go watch Netflix or have a beer with a friend and get on with your life. We can theorize about how and when to start the process (this book is full of that).

We can consider how to overcome a block or just plain lethargy, but in the end you cannot avoid the point when you just have to sit down and do something.

Before you actually start working, everything is a vision or an idea. You have not created anything. At the very most, you have thought of something you might create. But every single thing you do when you actually start to work is in essence the creative process.

"Creation is execution, not inspiration."
– Jimmy Carr

Creation includes practical tasks that might not seem that artistic when you look at them separately, such as making a list of the parts you need to write, writing an outline, or writing the opening scene, first verse, or just the first line of the verse. This is great news, because these are things you can do even if you are feeling uninspired.

As soon as you are writing something, there is also something to react to, to change, to rethink, to turn upside down, to inspire. You have knocked over the first domino.

Every masterpiece started with one sentence, one melody, one stroke of the paintbrush. There is absolutely no reason why this very moment could not be the moment where you start your masterpiece … or just start something!

"There never will be a better moment than this one, this one."
– Paul McCartney

WHAT HAVE YOU GOT TO LOSE?

No.4
What have you got to lose?

Writing nothing is not going to change anything. It will keep you right where you are, and stagnation is creativity's greatest enemy.

What is the worst thing that can happen? That you write something bad? That is still an improvement on your situation (see "Write something bad!").

DO YOUR JOB!

No.5
Do your job!

Have you heard of dentist's block, waitress's block, or pilot's block? I doubt it. But why does the concept seem so silly or unnatural? Maybe because the work of a dentist or a waitress seems so tangible. They have a specific job to do. Well, guess what? So do you!

The job of a songwriter, an author, or artist of any kind may seem kind of unspecific or fluffy, but it is really not. Avoiding writer's block is all about "doing".

Define the work: Focus on the process at hand and take it step by step instead of staring into the distance at a big blurry vision of all that this song or story could be.

Your actual job is the process. Do it!

WRITE SOMETHING BAD!

No.6
Write something bad!

When doing your job, whether it is taking meal orders, repairing teeth, or writing a novel, some days are going to be better than others. Some days you just have to punch in and do the work without necessarily aspiring to greatness.

Giving yourself permission to write something bad (but not permission to not write anything) is a good way to trick yourself into releasing the pressure. And yes, it's a trick because we rarely know for sure if something is good or bad until much later in the process anyway. "Bad" can be a starting point for greatness, just as well as we can mess something up that started as good or promising.

So, write something bad, something cheesy, something approaching plagiarism. Write whatever you think is possible today. If you finish it and still think it is bad, congratulate yourself. You have finished something! You have also practiced your craft, and maybe you just needed to get that bad stuff out of your system to make way for the next (great) thing.

NO EXCUSES

No.7
No excuses

Can you find time during the day to eat, go to the bathroom, drink some water? Of course you can. These are not just choices or hobbies, they are prioritized activities essential for a functioning human being on a daily basis. But they are also things that we can shuffle around in our schedule to some extent.

You can always find a reason not to write or convince yourself that something else is more important. But if you are serious about writing, you prioritize writing by putting it into the same category of importance as the other essentials.

There is always an excuse, but, more importantly, there is never an excuse!

BE A BEGINNER (EVERY TIME)

No.8
Be a beginner
(every time)

Beginners generally see joy in what they are doing. Why start doing something unless you think it will be fun or interesting?

A beginner is in the present, enjoying each step of the process without the weight of an inner critic or previous experience.
A beginner is also relatively unaware of risks and expectations and usually knows that challenges are teaching her "how to do", not telling her "not to do". She observes her own process with an open mind instead of blocking it.

Try to recapture a bit of "beginner's mind". Be curious about possibilities and observe the process as if you were watching from the outside (see also "Be an optimist"). Drop expectations and past experience and focus on the details of the process.

Leave your inner critic outside the door together with the vanity that steals your flow by comparing you to other writers or your own previous work.

Beginners dare to try something new - actually that is the only thing they can do. A beginner is in the moment because she does not know what lies beyond it, and neither do you even if you have tried it before.

A beginner has everything to gain and so do you, every time you start the creative process.

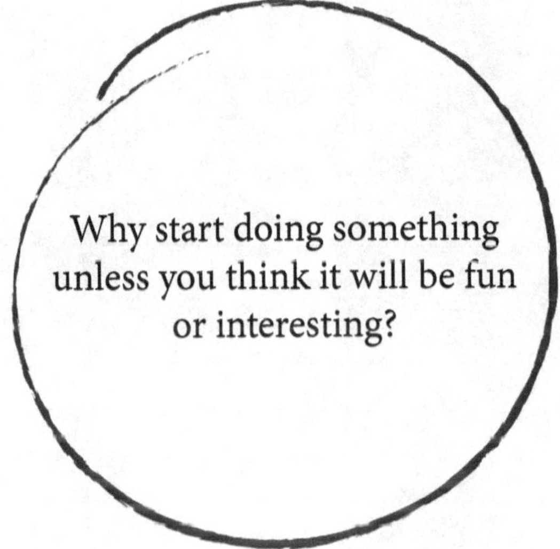
Why start doing something
unless you think it will be fun
or interesting?

ENJOY THE PROCESS

No.9
Enjoy the process

The process is the "doing" and the "being" of a writer. Finished and published stories, books, or songs are results. Hopefully, they are motivational milestones that build a career.

But as far as being an active writer goes, they actually mark each time you stop being a writer. Your real life as a writer is in the process.

That is not to say that some parts of the process can't be frustrating or even painful. The pain can make you and your final result better. That is why serious athletes are willing to endure pain. They know that pushing themselves to the limit of their abilities (and past) is what improves those abilities in the long run (no pun intended). This is also the case for a writer in the creative process!

Identify the pain

Sometimes this pain is not about the actual process at all. It can be caused by removing yourself from the present and worrying about things beyond the actual process or letting your ego get in the way (see "Write for yourself"). This is not the productive kind of pain. Park these thoughts until you are finished and concentrate on the present: the process.

Doing the work is being in the process and that is often a symbiosis of pain and pleasure. It is a productive balance where the pain builds the pleasure and vice versa.

Enjoy it!

The process is what makes
you a writer.

USE YOUR SUPERPOWERS

No. 10
Use your superpowers

… patience and persistence!

In the long run, moderately talented but hardworking writers very often outperform the wildly talented but undisciplined or lazy writers, because most of the creative process is "doing the work". Putting in the hours again and again improves your craft and also optimizes the odds of creating good stuff by creating more stuff.

And the great news about these superpowers (patience and persistence) is that everyone has access to them.

"Talent is only the starting point."
– Irving Berlin

You can be lucky to have a spurt of inspired creativity strike you out of the blue. Maybe you are channeling something that feels like it is writing itself without you having to do any conscious work? Bob Dylan said that "every grain of sand" came to him in this way.

It is amazing when it happens. And it might happen once a month or once in a lifetime, but this scenario is way too unreliable to base a career on.

"Thankfully, perseverance is a great substitute for talent."
– Steve Martin

Aesop's fable of the tortoise and the hare is very applicable when it comes to writing. Consistency triumphs over rushed work and ego-driven laziness. This applies to the process for a specific piece of work (e.g., a book or a song), but it is just as relevant (and maybe even more) the further we stretch the timeframe. This can be the difference between having and not having a career as a writer.

Time heals and also heals writer's block. But only time spent working on the creative process. This work fills the space that writer's block would otherwise grow in.

SHOW UP AND INSPIRATION WILL TOO

No.11
Show up and inspiration will too

Treating writing professionally also means showing up to work in the same way you would at any other place of work. As soon as you have shown up, you are making yourself actively available to the inspiration and ideas that will drive your process forward.

You are also removing the pressure of relying on freak occurrences of inspiration and the subsequent frantic scramble to make use of them.

"I only write when inspiration strikes. Fortunately, it strikes at nine every morning."
– William Faulkner

Sometimes ideas may not appear immediately or even after hours of work. But time and effort put into writing are never wasted.

Think of it as making a deposit to an inspirational savings account. The hours put in pay off even though it may happen later and out of context: in the shower, on the bus, or on a walk (see "Take a walk").

Every time you sit down and start working, you set in motion a new creative butterfly effect.

Every time you sit down
and start working, you set
in motion a new creative
butterfly effect.

DON'T WAIT FOR THE PERFECT TIME OR CONDITIONS

No.12
Don't wait for the perfect time or conditions

If you think that you need the right mood, the right desk, the perfect coffee, music, silence, coalition of stars, etc., you are making it very difficult to start work and giving yourself an endless list of reasons to avoid being creative.

"Waiting for the perfect conditions can postpone your work indefinitely."
– Scott Pack (in Tips from a Publisher)

If you want to be a writer, then you have to find a way to do that in your everyday life with all the distractions, noises, mood swings, and bad coffee that may imply.

In art, there are no wrong feelings, no wrong time, or wrong conditions. If the conditions do not feel right, change what you are writing to fit them.

As a writer, you are a mirror of your time. Sometimes, a moment in time will encapsulate one feeling, sometimes the very opposite is true, but no feeling is worth more or less than others.

Very few people only want to write (or let alone read) about only one feeling, and that's what you are trying to do by confining your "creative time" to one specific scenario. Let your creative conditions and output vary like life itself.

If you want to be a writer,
then you have to find a way
to do that in your everyday
life with all the distractions
that may imply.

DON'T WAIT FOR
THE PERFECT IDEA

No.13
Don't wait for the perfect idea

… or even a good idea!

Generally, an idea is just … an idea. You are the one who can make it good or perfect with work, craft, and time. There is no sense in judging it before you have done the work. That is like judging a cake by tasting raw flour and eggs.

Take the idea you have and put in the effort to make it great, step by step. Because the alternative is an idea you do not have—and you can't do anything with that.

MAKE A CHOICE!

No.14
Make a choice!

Sometimes the problem is not a lack of choices, it is having too many! With every step of the creative process, there are options and decisions to be made.

Don't worry about all the options you discard. Making a piece of art is not about trying to include all possible aspects of a certain story or emotion, it is actually about zooming in and focusing on one main one. Keeping too many options open during the process usually results in an unclear result.

PS. If you are having a hard time making choices, give yourself a hard deadline (see "Deadlines"). If you only have limited time to get something done, you cannot pursue all possible directions.

IF IT DOESN'T WORK, CHANGE IT

No.15
If it doesn't work, change it

If you are stuck banging your head against the same wall (or same writer's block), it makes no sense continuing to check into the same scenario. This only becomes self-reinforcing proof of your creative failure.

"Insanity is doing the same thing over and over again and expecting different results."
– Albert Einstein

To change the result (or lack thereof), you must change the process.

For example:

Change the "where": If you usually write at home, then go to a café, library, or the park.

Change the "when": If you usually write in the evening, try in the morning.

Change the "how": This could be the order in which you do things or the way you do them (get inspiration from some of the chapters in this book and explore other people's process in books or online and give them a shot).

To change the result, you
must change the process.

BE AN OPTIMIST

No.16
Be an optimist

To create, you have to focus on the best-case scenario. You must look for possibilities and solutions. You are on a creative climb, reaching to grab hold of the next branch and pull yourself further up.

Do not second guess ideas unless you have an alternative option to replace what you are cutting down. If you focus on the fall instead of the climb, you will miss valuable lifelines and end up falling.

"The professional keeps his eye on the doughnut and not on the hole."
– Steven Pressfield (The War of Art)

These potential holes and blocks are the actual fabric of writer's block. A productive process is a constant slalom between and around them.

PURSUE DUMB IDEAS!

No.17
Pursue dumb ideas!

The only way you can be sure of avoiding "dumb ideas" is by only doing what you already know and can. And that is really dumb! Throughout history, most pioneers and first movers were initially ridiculed for their ideas.

In 1630, Galileo was thrown into prison by the Catholic Church for declaring that the Earth revolved around the sun when the Earth was obviously "the center of the universe".

In 1876, the telegraph company Western Union passed on a new invention called the telephone with the words "the device is inherently of no value to us".

And when silent movies were challenged by the new technology of synchronized audio in 1928 the president of United Artists commented to the New York Times that synchronized audio was a gimmick that would not last.

It can take time to understand or accept new ideas, because new ideas can often seem inconvenient or even dangerous by challenging accepted preconceptions.

The same mechanisms can arise as an inner dialogue when you consider whether an idea is worth pursuing or if it is just "dumb".

In these situations, consider whether the idea is truly dumb or not (is it a dead end or does it open doors to other ideas?). Maybe you are being lazy because the idea is outside your comfort zone, or maybe you are scared because the idea is controversial?

In both cases, the answer is the same: Pursue that idea!

Some people equate "dumb" with "high risk", but there is a difference. Taking chances by exploring uncharted territory in the creative process is not dumb, it is often downright necessary!

And no, not all unusual ideas will change the world or even lead to a good creative product. But they can be the steppingstone to the next idea, which might just be the one you were looking for.

By allowing room for dumb ideas, we open doors to new possibilities and simply optimize the odds of creating something good.

Do not let the fear of doing something dumb hold you back from new, unknown creative adventures.

BE GRATEFUL

No.18
Be grateful

If you are reading this book, you are probably one of the luckiest people on Earth! Not (only) because you have this book, but you apparently have the great privilege of having time to create, to ponder creativity, and even to read my thoughts on the matter.

It is unlikely that you are going to starve if you don't write something or if you write something bad. You can do it just because you want to and because it fascinates you.

Around a billion people on our planet are living in extreme poverty, spending all their waking hours just trying to survive. But no matter what the outcome of your creativity, you have the opportunity to spend time writing.

So do it, you lucky bastard!

SNAPSHOTS FROM A WRITER'S LIFE

No.19
Snapshots from a writer's life

On a certain day, you may have planned to write something funny and quirky but for some reason it is just not happening. Your mind is in a darker place.

Do not try to force the flow of your creativity into a direction to "stick to the plan". The unexpected direction is the new plan. Today is not your once in a lifetime make-or-break shot at writing. Writing is an ongoing pursuit that will provide many other days and moods.

Consider every day of writing a snapshot from a day in the life of a writer.

Challenging times of life crisis, loss, divorce, heartbreak, etc. are not necessarily things that get in the way of your writing. They are actually the very things that warrant your writing—meaningful emotional events and experiences to be documented or to color the filter through which you are writing something (something that may have nothing to do with the current life crisis).

You can only ever write the best possible thing on the given day, in the given mindset, under the given circumstances. And that is actually your job as a writer reporting from the frontline of your life.

You can only write the best
possible thing on the given day,
under the given circumstances.

WRITING IS WHAT YOU DO, NOT WHO YOU ARE!

No.20
Writing is what you do, not who you are!

"Oh, but my writing only comes from the heart blah blah blah …".

Hopefully, a lot of your writing does come from the heart, but your writing is not your heart.

We like to equate writers with their writing. To most fans, Paul McCartney is actually lamenting his own lost love directly in "Yesterday", and Charles Bukowski is the drunken Hank Chinaski from his novels. As consumers, that is exactly what we should believe.

McCartney and Bukowski are most certainly writing what they know, inspired by real locations, people, feelings, and experience. But every novel, song, or film is a piece of art, a product, or whatever you want to call it, that has been worked on, structured, written, sometimes re-written, and completed in some form.

It is not an actual part of the creator's body that has magically dropped out of their head or elbow and assumed the form of a book or vinyl record.

Even though you may feel that you are giving birth to a part of yourself when you are struck by inspiration or hit the perfect rhythm in a flow state, you are still a separate entity forming and filtering the art. That does not mean it is not personal, meaningful, and full of your artistic fingerprints.

The art is separate from the artist. This is very helpful to remember when you are finding it hard to create or when receiving harsh critique— especially self-critique. Do not take it personally. It is not you, it is the piece of work, and luckily that can be changed and improved.

You can stick with it or you can let it go and accept it as the snapshot of the day (see the chapter "Snapshots from a writer's life").

You are not an eternally amazing person because you have created something amazing, and you are not eternally useless because you have written something bad.

Your writing is not you.

DON'T BE ORIGINAL

No.21
Don't be
original

If someone actually created a truly 100% original work of art, something that had never been portrayed before and in a way never done before, I am guessing that it would be more of a scientific novelty than an emotional experience.

What we relate to, what makes us cry, laugh, or feel inspired is not original. It is a handful of universal themes consisting of the same feelings and life experiences that everyone on Earth goes through in their own context.

Writers are recyclers. If your frame of reference is wide enough, you can always find something similar or even a direct (although maybe unconscious) inspiration. Your writing is a product of all the books, films, songs, etc. you have digested and poured through a filter of your own taste, life, and skillset.

"Those who do not want to imitate anything, produce nothing." – Salvador Dali

As long as your angle is inspiring and driving your work forward, don't let concerns or ambitions of originality get in the way of your writing. Using somebody else's work as a reference or inspiration can be a great way of getting a focused start to your writing.

Chances are that your writing is going to take turns and detours that turn it into something different anyway.

Writers are recyclers

DON'T BE THE BEST, DO YOUR BEST

No.22
Don't be the best, do your best

With the Internet, e-books, streaming, audio-books, etc., you have access to all the greatest books, songs, and films of all time, any time. This can be inspiring, but it can also be overwhelming. In the worst case, it can steal your motivation to create anything.

Most things you start will seem feeble and lacking in comparison to the masterpieces of the hardest working geniuses in history. And they probably are!

"Comparison is the thief of joy."
– Theodore Roosevelt

But remember that when you compare what you are creating with what they have created, the comparison is way off balance. First off, you are comparing a work-in-progress with finished results. Results that are usually the product of multiple drafts, rewrites, finetuning, scrutinizing, or just the most inspired minutes of a lifetime.

We love stories of the artist being possessed by inspiration and channeling a masterpiece almost unconsciously. Paul McCartney dreamt the melody for "Yesterday", and Jack Kerouac allegedly typed out On the Road on one continuous reel of paper in only three weeks. But even these flashes of genius are generally the product of a long list of preceding results that were uninteresting to the world until the writer finally "got it right" (see "Show up and inspiration will too").

Usually, a relevant prologue is omitted. For example, Kerouac actually filled a stack of notebooks with what would be the core of On the Road in the years before he sat down to write it. And McCartney spent years learning to craft and structure songs before he and Lennon found a method that would write history.

J.K. Rowling allegedly rewrote the first chapter of The Sorcerer's Stone over 15 times, and Leonard Cohen spent 5 years and an estimated 80 drafts on getting "Hallelujah" right (check out Malcolm Gladwell's podcast Revisionist History on how genius emerges).

Don't waste time and block yourself by comparing yourself to the best. The best? What is that anyway? The best at writing what, for who?

You are the only person you should be comparing yourself to. Be better than you were last time. The rest of the world can do the comparing when you are done doing your very best.

"There is nothing noble in being superior to your fellow men. True nobility lies in being superior to your former self."
– Ernest Hemingway

THE WHOLE WORLD DOESN'T GIVE A SHIT!

No.23
The whole world doesn't give a shit!

… unless what you have created is exceptional!

Most mediocrity or rubbish flies under the radar (unfortunately sometimes good stuff does too!). So, there is no point in stressing about expectations. Those expectations are probably somewhere between nonexistent and a lot less than you (or your ego) would like to believe.

If what you are working on is, in fact, a piece of garbage, then most of the world will never find out and the upside is that you got it out of your system (see "Write something bad!"). So, write what you want to and what feels good to you (see "Write for yourself").

MAKE DEADLINES (BIG AND SMALL)

No.24
Make deadlines (big and small)

Without structure, the creative process can be prolonged indefinitely. Challenges can grow into walls looming over you, paralyzing your progress. Deadlines force you to structure your time and work. This promotes finding solutions. And the creative process is basically a string of solutions leading to a final product.

It is hard to travel without a destination, but it does not have to be the final destination. The thought of your final creative destination may be overwhelming to consider at the starting line, so divide the work into steps, each with their own deadline.

Make sure these deadlines are realistic – it is better that they are too easy than too ambitious. It feels a lot better to get ahead of an easy deadline than to get behind a tight deadline.

SCHEDULE
AND FORGET

No.25
Schedule
and forget

Things you need to do can follow you around like a black cloud. They become a constant stress factor and distraction while you are doing other things. This is not constructive. It just drains you and makes you feel exhausted before you even get the chance to give the work a shot.

To avoid this, you must confront those tasks. There are two choices:

1) Do it now (see "Do something … now!")
2) Do not do it now.

Deciding not to do it now is actually proactive and you are taking initiative. However, it also entails two more questions that you must face:

1) Are you going to do it at all?
2) When are you going to do it?

If you go with option 2 again, then schedule time in your calendar when you will do the work. If there are multiple things, then make multiple "dates" in your schedule just as you would if they were different people you had meetings with.

Once you have parked these nagging "to-dos", allow yourself to enjoy your free time or time to work on other things without worrying about unfinished tasks. They are now scheduled. Hopefully, you will get to them without feeling tired and drained before you even start. Ideas will often start popping up before your scheduled timeslot because they are no longer forced.

Do it now
or
do not do it now

TAKE A WALK

No.26
Take a walk

The creative process seems to alternate between two phases. One is a free-flowing chaos of ideas and unconscious inspiration. The other is a more craft-driven phase of editing, structuring, and focus.

In the TV series Mad Men, set in the Manhattan advertising world of the 1950s, adman extraordinaire Don Draper gives his protégé, Peggy, her first assignment. After pitching numerous ideas in vain, she is on the verge of giving up. Don tells her that she needs to think about it, long and hard, and forget about it. Then the right idea will pop up. That, in all its simplicity, is often the case.

Who hasn't had a great idea in the shower, on a bus, or at night as you lay in bed and let your thoughts fly?

It seems as if ideas and solutions to creative challenges show up randomly and often inconveniently. But what generally happens is that you have put in the preliminary work, investing time in finding a direction for your thoughts and creative flow. Those thoughts continue to simmer unconsciously in your mind and then send a message to the surface when they have a solution.

Disconnecting and letting go is just as important as concentrating and working. Sometimes we need to shut off the conscious creation to make space for new ideas or solutions to creative challenges to bloom.

One of the best ways to take a time-out and give the unconscious mind space to work is by walking. No AirPods with music, no checking smartphones, just walking and being.

"All truly great thoughts are conceived
by walking."
– Friedrich Nietzsche

No AirPods with music,
no checking smartphones,
just walking and being.

DANCE WITH THE MAGIC

No.27
Dance with the magic

When you're in a flow state, writing can feel effortless. On rare occasions, you might get lucky and complete what you are working on in a blinding flash of pure flow or inspiration or whatever you call "the magic".

But most of the time, the creative process will alternate between the magic and more hands-on phases of "work and effort". Keeping that interaction going for as long as possible is essential to the creative process.

It is like a dance, a dance with the magic. And you and the magic cannot both lead at the same time. When the magic leads, it will feel effortless, but when it stops you must take the lead. Grab hold and lead step by step. In this phase, you can control starting points, structure, plans, etc.

When the next steps start to feel less and less obvious and the dance slows down, it is important to let go and create space for the magic. If you do this before you are completely drained, you will not hit a stop sign if the magic only takes the lead for a minute. And a full stop is the worst starting point for a dance with the magic.

We are not trying to take control of this magic, inspiration, or flow. We are trying to continually maneuver ourselves into the current of the flow.

"I just get out of the way and then it comes."
– Sia (on melody in Louis Theroux's podcast Grounded)

It is like a dance, a dance
with the magic.
And you cannot both lead
at the same time.

BE PREPARED
TO BE IMPULSIVE

No.28
Be prepared to be impulsive!

Most of my best work did not come from ideas I prepared beforehand but things that arose in the moment.

Irresistibly inspiring ideas are rarely found on standby in a notebook, Word file, or voice memo on your phone. When they pop up, you must follow them into dark, dangerous, untrodden pathways leading deeper into the jungle of creation.

This does not mean that you should wait passively for the magic to appear. Practice and preparation give you the skills and the courage to optimize your chances of catching the magic.

So, by all means, collect ideas, make plans, use proven techniques, backup ideas and starting points, but be prepared to throw everything aside and go with an impulse.

Because if you never take chances, you will only continue repeating what you already know.

REACH OUT!

No.29
Reach out!

Involving others in your creative process is a great way of getting things moving. Co-writing is the most obvious. Having two minds and someone else's thoughts and ideas to react to when you hit a wall should have the potential for a never-ending ping-pong.

Meeting up with someone else also makes it an occasion that can be motivational in that you are physically moving yourself to the co-writing situation with a focus on creating. You are also making yourself and your writing accountable to others, which is a good antidote to procrastination.

If you are not into co-creativity, you can still nudge your writing by making yourself accountable to others. Ask someone to read what you have written by a certain deadline and give you their feedback. Or tell a close friend or partner that you are buying them dinner if you have not completed a certain writing task by a specific deadline.

WRITE FOR YOURSELF

No.30
Write for yourself

… even if you are writing for someone else.

Do not think about what others will think about your work, what the reviews will be like, who will think you are cool and who will not. This is your ego getting in the way of the work.

Your ego focuses on your value in other people's eyes, not on the value of your work in its own right. You are moving the work away from what you know: your judgement, taste, etc. and in that terrain, everything is guess-work.

As a songwriter, I have put words into the mouths of many known singers. Often, they will have a whole list of dos and don'ts about lyrical content, but the best results (and what has made them happiest) have always been when I have written what I would like to hear them sing. This realization gives me "artistic confidence".

What you want to write most will usually be what you write best. So, it only seems logical to allow yourself some confidence regarding your artistic choices in this context.

What is important is conveying what you want to communicate in a way that people will understand. Their opinion on the way you do this is out of your control and has nothing to do with the work at hand right now.

"Be who you are and say what
you feel because those who
mind don't matter and those
who matter don't mind."
– Dr. Suess

REMIND YOURSELF OF "THAT FEELING"

No.31
Remind yourself of "that feeling"

Completing even small parts of a project can be incredibly motivational. Remind yourself of that great feeling waiting for you on the other side of your next deadline or task (see "Deadlines").

Take a moment to congratulate yourself with every completed step in the process. Savor the satisfaction and use it to make you feel positive about engaging with the next part of the work that will once again lead you to this satisfaction—a feeling that will accumulate as you get closer to your project's final destination.

AT THE
FINISHING LINE

No.32
At the finishing line

As long as what you are writing is a "work in progress", the potential is limitless. You could be writing a masterpiece, a new "Yesterday" or Harry Potter. So, approaching the finishing line can feel like a dangerous place. Because this is the point where "all that it could be" becomes "what it is" and where we have to take responsibility for the finished product.

Basic statistics imply that the more projects you finish, the higher the chance of actually making that masterpiece. At the same time, it brings a natural acceptance of the fact that everything you finish is not going to be a masterpiece.

And that's okay! Actually, it is good, because that acceptance releases pressure that manifests itself as writer's block early in the process (see "Do your job" and "Do something now").

Not finishing is creative cowardice! It is like being a soccer striker but never actually taking a shot at the goal. It reduces your creativity to a hobby, purely for your own enjoyment.

Finished work is the only work that exists to the outside world. Therefore, your completed novels, songs, or stories are the blocks that build your career and define you as an artist.

Not finishing is creative
cowardice!

FINISHED ...
FOR NOW

No.33
Finished ...
for now

Completed work is not necessarily finished. This seems contradictory to the previous chapter, but completing something means making the best final version possible at this point in time. That doesn't mean that you cannot revisit it and make it even better later on if the right idea arises.

You are completing it for now. But more often than not, you will find that it was in fact final.

There is a big difference though between completing a version of something and leaving something unfinished and open. Finishing projects is a skill in itself. And this skill is just as important to practice as any other part of the creative process.

AFTERTHOUGHT

Afterthought

Having problems finishing a book on writer's block would have been a perfectly comedic situation!

Luckily, this was not the case. Instead, a positive meta-situation arose, making this book a case in point on avoiding writer's block.

I have written four books before this one, and often the process seemed laborious, long, and slow—especially compared to the more compact process of writing 3-minute pop songs, the creative process I have predominantly been accustomed to for the last 25 years.

This book actually sped past the other two books I am currently working on. So it was worth reflecting on why. And now that I have, these experiences have given my other book projects a very productive kick in the ass!

So, what did I do while writing "Unblock your writing"? Early on, I decided to allow myself only short periods of time to work on the book, since it was "only" a side project. Sometimes only a couple of minutes to jot down an idea for a new chapter or elaborate on a chapter in progress.

Every potential pitfall in the writing process was also a new chapter. When I started worrying about how this book might be received, instead of letting those thoughts become a block they became the chapter "Write for yourself". When I couldn't figure out if a chapter was finished or not, I wrote "Finished … for now".

Whenever I finished a chapter, I made myself jot down a few lines, ideas, or just words for a new chapter. So, there was always at least one open door, one pre-prepared idea when the new ones were not flowing.

I used the writing program Scrivener and always had the project open on my laptop so that I could access my project quickly before having my attention hijacked by an email or Facebook. As the chapters grew, they became a list of what I needed to remember in order to keep the process moving forward.

Writer's block is not something that you get "cured" of by reading a book. It is an ongoing process of learning to separate your creativity from artistic self-doubt, ego mind tricks, and all their ugly friends without letting them take control—much like the principle of meditation, where you detach yourself from your thoughts by observing them and letting them pass.

I hope that my thoughts and suggestions help you find the mindset that works for you.

Now go and write something!

about the author

Englishborn Marcus Winther-John began his career in music as leadsinger in the wellknown danish 90's rockband, Inside the Whale, releasing 4 albums on Sony Music, Denmark.

After the band split up Marcus started a succesful career writing for a long list of gold and platinum certified releases with rock, pop and country artsts in Denmark.

The list of international artists is just as long including K-pop giants SHINee and Red Velvet, US boyband legends New Kids on the Block, Spanish superstar David Bisbal and many other established artists in Sweden, Germany, Spain etc.

Marcus' songs have also been placed in film and tv such as The Vampire Diaries, Lego Friends, Ramasjang (Danish national tv's children's channel), the Disney tween-series Violetta (65 songs!), two X-factor winnersongs and local and international finalists for the Eurovision Song Contest in Sweden, Denmark, Spain, Andorra, Belgium and Cyprus.

Marcus also teaches songwriting at the Royal Academy of Music and Danish Songwriting Academy in Denmark and debuted as an author with the songwriting book "Skriv Hits & Sælg Dem" in 2017 and has since also released his debut novel "16 Hangovers" and two music biographies.

Marcus lives in Copenhagen with his two sons.

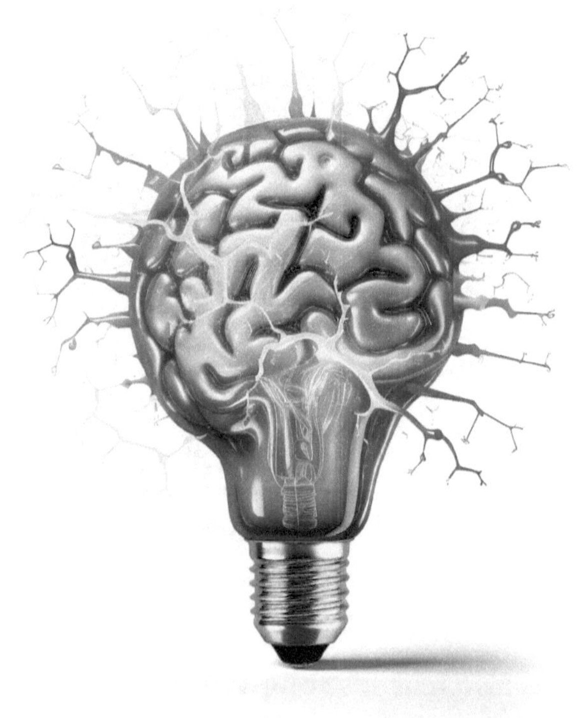

*

by the same author
"16 hangovers" - 2023

Follow Marcus at
Instagram @write.hits

www.ingramcontent.com/pod-product-compliance
Lightning Source LLC
Chambersburg PA
CBHW031308250726

48656CB00005B/1693